BOB LOVES VOLCANOES

including

The Legend of the Mountains

N. Scrantz Lersch

For permission contact:

Studio 37
Portland, Oregon
Madison, Wisconsin
USA
at
scrantz@gmail.com

Bob Loves Volcanoes
1. Volcano geology 2. Volcano legend 3. Pacific Northwest 4. Mount Hood
5. Mount St. Helens 6. Mount Adams 7. Oregon volcanoes
8. Washington Volcanoes 9. Native American Legend
10. Mt. Rainier 11. Loowit, Pahtoe, Wy'east

Studio 37 Publications
502 Leonard Street
Madison, Wisconsin 53711

ISBN-13: 978-0615923291
ISBN-10: 0615923291

For everyone who likes to go
walking on volcanoes with me

Dedicated to
Scientists who study things,
including volcanoes

Bob woke up every morning and looked out
his window. On sunny days he could see
a beautiful white mountain.

It was a VOLCANO.

Bob was very curious.

He wondered how VOLCANOES were formed.

He learned that volcanoes
are created when
molten or melted rock
comes out from
inside the Earth
through a crack or a vent
in the Earth's crust.

The molten rock
is called
MAGMA.

When the magma flows out
from the underground
it is called
LAVA.

Bob learned that the tall cone-shaped volcano that he could see was called a STRATOVOLCANO. "Strato" means layer.

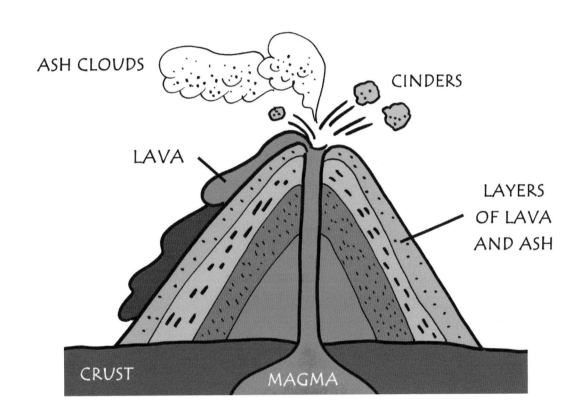

STRATOVOLCANOES are formed when the lava flows out of the vent. Then cinders and ash pile on top. Then more lava flows on top of the cinders and ash. The lava becomes solid rock very quickly as it reaches the air. This happens again and again, forming layers.

Sometimes the lava BURSTS out of the vent! This is called a VOLCANIC ERUPTION. Mountains are created when volcanoes erupt over tens and hundreds of thousands of years.

Bob learned that volcanoes are found all over our planet EARTH.

He discovered that there are MANY volcanoes erupting EVERY day, somewhere on our planet!

Bob discovered that volcanoes can be ACTIVE, DORMANT or EXTINCT.

A volcano is ACTIVE when
lava, steam or ash is
coming out of the vent.

A DORMANT volcano is sleeping.
It has erupted in recent history, but now is quiet.

EXTINCT volcanoes have had
no activity in historical times
and are unlikely to erupt again.

Bob found that there are volcanoes
UNDER the oceans!
These are called SUBMARINE VOLCANOES.

"SUB" means under. "MARINE" means ocean or sea.

The LARGEST volcano on earth, TAMU MASSIF,
is entirely under the ocean!
It is located about a thousand miles east of Japan
in the northwestern Pacific Ocean.

Bob learned that TAMU MASSIF
is a SHIELD VOLCANO
and has been extinct for millions of years.

SHIELD VOLCANOES, like
TAMU MASSIF, form layer by layer as
fast-moving lava flows
from a central vent in all directions.
The lava runs down the volcano's flanks,
and cools in place.

Bob's friend, Julie,
likes to go visit HAWAII
and go swimming!

Bob learned that the
Hawaiian Islands
are also
SHIELD VOLCANOES.

They were formed when
underwater volcanoes
erupted over
millions of years
and grew so tall
that the tops
of the mountains came
above the sea level.

Hawaii became the
50th state of the
United States of America
in 1959.

Bob learned that there are many volcanoes
in Washington and Oregon.

He discovered that his Grandma Shen climbed
Mount Rainier when she was in college!
It is a volcano in Washington State
and is called TAHOMA by Native Americans.
It is 14,410 feet high (4,392 meters).

When volcanoes and mountains are measured, they are measured from sea level. When we say a mountain is 14,000 feet "high" we mean that the top, or SUMMIT, is 14,000 feet above sea level.

Bob learned that Mount Hood is a dormant volcano located in the state of Oregon.
It is 11,250 feet high (3,429 meters).

He discovered that Mount Adams is a dormant volcano in Washington State.
Mount Adams is 12,280 feet high (3,743 meters).

Bob learned that
Mount St. Helens is an active volcano
located in Washington State.

In the spring of 1980, Mount St. Helens started to
tremble and rumble with earthquakes.

On May 17, 1980, the mountain was
9,677 feet high (2,950 meters).

On the morning of May 18, 1980, there was a
MASSIVE ERUPTION.
The eruption produced huge ash clouds and
avalanches of rocks and mud.
Millions of trees were blown over.

After this eruption the mountain was
only 8,365 feet high (2,550 meters).
Mount St. Helens last erupted between
2004 and 2008.

Bob and his friend, Javier,
discovered that the Native American people
who first lived near these mountains
had different names for these volcanoes.
They called them
Loowit, Pahtoe and Wy'east.

Bob and Javier like to go to the top of
Rocky Butte in Portland, Oregon.
From the top they can see these
THREE volcanoes!

Bob and Javier learned that about
two hundred years ago, when European explorers first
sailed their ships up the rivers of the Northwest, they
gave new names to these mountains.

Loowit was renamed Mount St. Helens
by Captain George Vancouver when
he was surveying the northern Pacific coast
in his ship Discovery.
He named it for British diplomat
Baron St. Helens in 1792.

Wy'east was renamed Mount Hood for
British Admiral Samuel Hood.

Pahtoe was renamed Mount Adams in 1839
for President John Adams, by Hall J. Kelly.

Javier and Bob also found that
Native American people had a LEGEND, a story,
about how these mountains were formed.

A LEGEND is a traditional story passed down
from generation to generation.

The Legend of the Mountains

Fifteen thousand years ago, two groups of native people lived alongside a great river. They called themselves the Multnomah and Klickitat people.
Their Great Spirit was called Sahale.

As was the custom of the river people,
the young men and boys were always busy
fishing for salmon and hunting for deer and elk.
The women and girls collected berries and worked
alongside each other to smoke the salmon
so it would last through the winter.

Wy'east, a young man of the Multnomah people, was
well known for catching hundreds of salmon every year
when the fish would leap up the rapids.

A young Klickitat man, Pahtoe,
was famous for his skill at being very quiet
in the forest and hunting elk and deer.

Loowit was a beautiful young woman who lived near the river. She worked with her mother, sisters and cousins picking berries, drying fish and gathering herbs for medicines and cooking.
She also wove beautiful baskets from reeds and grass to carry the berries and plants.

Wy'east and Pahtoe always came to admire her new baskets. Wy'east loved Loowit. Pahtoe also loved her. Time passed and Loowit could not decide which of the handsome young men she liked better so the two men began to quarrel.

Wy'east and Pahtoe fought over her. They stomped their feet and caused the earth to tremble and rumble. They threw fiery rocks across the river at each other, burying villages and forests.

The Great Spirit Sahale was furious!
He commanded the young men to STOP
their quarreling and solve their problems.
But they were not able to stop fighting.

Sahale cast a spell on the three young people and
changed each into a mighty mountain.
The lovely Loowit became a beautiful,
symmetrical cone of dazzling white.

Pahtoe wept to see
Loowit wrapped in snow.
He bent his head as he gazed on her
and his rounded shoulders form
the top of his mountain.

But Wy'east lifted his head in pride
and has a great pointed top.

The End

Bob discovered that he wanted to know more about volcanoes and decided that he would learn as much as he could about volcanoes just for fun!

He learned that the LARGEST volcano in the entire SOLAR SYSTEM is on the PLANET MARS! It is a shield volcano called OLYMPUS MONS, and measures 69,649 feet (21,229 meters), almost 14 miles high!

He learned that there are over 130 active volcanoes, in the country of INDONESIA, more than in any other country on Earth!

Bob read that in Italy, the volcano
MOUNT VESUVIUS erupted in 79 AD.
Ash from that eruption completely
buried a town called POMPEII.

Archaeologists have been digging out
this Roman town for over 250 years!
They have found streets, houses, shops and theaters.

He learned that in the countries of
Rwanda and Uganda, in Africa,
there are volcanoes where mountain gorillas live!

Bob discovered that in Antarctica
there are both active and extinct volcanoes.
Mt Erebus, an active volcano near the South Pole,
has a LAVA LAKE in the crater at its summit!

A LAVA LAKE is created when molten lava erupts from inside
the Earth and collects in a crater or depression.

He learned that there are scientists who study volcanoes.
They are called VOLCANOLOGISTS.

Bob thinks that HE might become a
volcanologist someday!

DRAW A VOLCANO HERE!

About the Author

N. Scrantz Lersch likes to draw pictures,
read books and play outside whenever she can.
This is a picture of her hiking in Oregon
near the volcanoes known as the Three Sisters.

29509064R00023

Made in the USA
Charleston, SC
17 May 2014